MW00881161

HELLO!

THIS BOOK BELONGS TO

This edition was published by The Dreamwork Collective
The Dreamwork Collective LLC, Dubai, United Arab Emirates
thedreamworkcollective.com

Printed and bound by Al Ghurair Printing Press in the United Arab Emirates

www.girlsdogood.co
josdirkx.com

ISBN 978-9948-39-644-4

Approved by National Media Council
Dubai, United Arab Emirates
MF-02-2316849

Author: Jos Dirkx
Cover and Book Design: Jade Isaks
Illustrations: Bianca De Jong
Editor: Thalia Suzuma

Generous support for this publication was provided by Huda Beauty hudabeauty.com

Disclaimer

We would like to thank the girls portrayed in this book for allowing their stories to be recounted by the author. The world-changing ideas featured in the stories are the intellectual property of the girls featured. Although the author and publisher have made every effort to ensure that the information in this book was correct at press time, the author and publisher do not assume and hereby disclaim any liability to any party for any loss, damage, or disruption caused by errors or omissions, whether such errors or omissions result from negligence, accident, or any other cause. For more information on the sources used to develop the stories, please visit www.girlsdogood.co.

WHO INSPIRES YOU?

MY MOM.

3rd grade, circa 1995
Madrid, Spain

To my real-life superhero, my mother.

LEYMAH GBOWEE

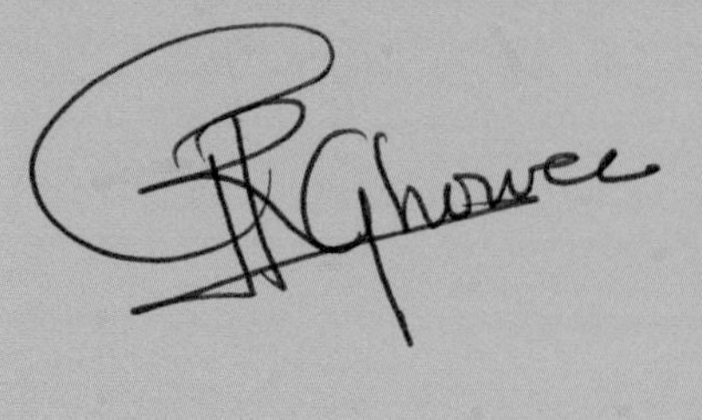

Nobel Peace Prize Winner, Founder of Gbowee Peace Foundation Africa

I had just finished high school when war broke out in my country of Liberia. I studied as a social worker so that I could help the women and children who were hurt. But it wasn't enough, I knew we had to stop the war so that we could all be safe. We gathered the women together to pray and we worked together for peace. It took time, but our efforts succeeded. The war ended.

When I think back on our movement for peace, one of the most powerful tools we had were our voices and our stories. I have a dream for the girls of Liberia and for every girl around the world — that she can go to school, that she will know herself, and that she knows how to use her voice to stand up for herself and her community.

All around the world, girls are identifying things that they want to change. The stories in *Girls Do Good* are just a snapshot of the creativity and problem-solving abilities of girls.

Girls — use your voice, stand strong in your values, and look out for your fellow sisters. Never give up, and press for excellence in all that you do.

HUDA KATTAN

Beauty Blogger and Entrepreneur
CEO of Huda Beauty

I grew up in an itty bitty town in the United States where no one really looked like me. I always felt like I didn't fit in and thought that by being different, maybe there was something wrong with me — I remember being called weird all the time and thinking, "Why can't I just be normal like everyone else?" I soon became obsessed with the art in beauty and found I could express myself through makeup. It helped me feel that maybe I was different in a special kind of way.

After years of falling in love with beauty and learning a lot, I decided I wanted to share my knowledge with the world! I wanted beauty to be something that everyone could feel and makeup became my tool for helping people achieve that.

I started blogging — writing and recording videos — to tell the world that maybe you're different for a reason, and that's wonderful! Makeup gave me the chance to feel understood and even appreciated, which lit a fire of confidence in me I had never had before — it was powerful.

My sister Mona gave me an idea. She made me see that even though I was doing good by changing the way people used makeup, maybe I could change the way people made it, too. Growing up, I couldn't find makeup that matched my skin color or suited my features, so I started creating makeup in all kind of colors, so people who looked different could find makeup that matched them, too. Now I run a business with my sisters, Mona and Alya, that shares all kinds of beauty with the world every single day.

I want every girl to know that what makes you different is what makes you beautiful. Owning and accepting that you are special before anyone else does can not only empower you, but others, too! If you love yourself, and just be yourself, you will change the world like all of the other girls in this book.

COLOR-IN

ONLINE

AND

BRING YOUR

STORIES

TO LIFE

USE YOUR PHONE TO SCAN THE QR CODE BELOW AND START YOUR DIGITAL JOURNEY.

Color the drawings in on your mobile device or tablet.

And bring images in this book to life using Augmented Reality!

Go to www.girlsdogood.co/explore to learn more.

REDEFINING 'GOOD'

DO YOU WANT TO CHANGE THE WORLD IN YOUR VERY OWN WAY?

--→ SO DO WE. ←--

A 'good' girl used to mean being a nice girl. A quiet girl. A girl who played by the rules, didn't speak up, and didn't challenge the system.

We are consciously choosing to re-write the narrative about the meaning of 'being good'. This is about your own version of good.

Girls aren't good. They aren't bad. They're girls. And we can all do our own version of good, just like these real-life superheroes, to change our world bit by bit.

MEET THE GIRLS

The Environmentalists

Melati (17) and Isabel (15), Indonesia

BYE BYE PLASTIC BAGS!

Hi! We are Isabel and Melati.

Isabel and Melati live on an island in Indonesia. People on their island use too many plastic bags. Plastic bags are a problem all around the world — not just in Indonesia — because they are bad for the environment.

Sometimes animals eat the plastic bags and they don't survive. The plastic bags litter many beaches.

Isabel and Melati were sad that animals were being harmed by the plastic bags. They also didn't like seeing their beaches looking dirty, so they started cleaning up. They picked up hundreds of plastic bags each week.

But they needed help. They spoke to the adults they knew and asked them to stop using plastic bags. They asked other kids to help them clean up the plastic bags, too.

Now kids on Indonesia's many islands, and all over the world, are helping keep our planet clean.

If you see a friend throw plastic on the ground, ask them, "Can you please put your rubbish in the trash can? Littering is bad for the environment."

DID YOU KNOW?

Nearly half of all seabirds in the world have either eaten or become entangled in plastic.

The Singer

Ashleigh (19), Ireland

SINGING WITH THE STARS

Hello! My name is Ashleigh.

Ashleigh can play music on her guitar, her harp and even on a tin whistle! But more than anything, Ashleigh loves to sing.

Ashleigh doesn't read or write music, so she taught herself to sing and play musical instruments by listening to songs and sounds.

"It takes me a few weeks to learn a song so I just sing it again and again," she says.

Ashleigh also has autism. Autism can make it hard to connect with people and to make new friends.

That is one of the reasons music is so important to Ashleigh.

"It makes me feel really happy," she says. "It's really nice that my music makes people feel good."

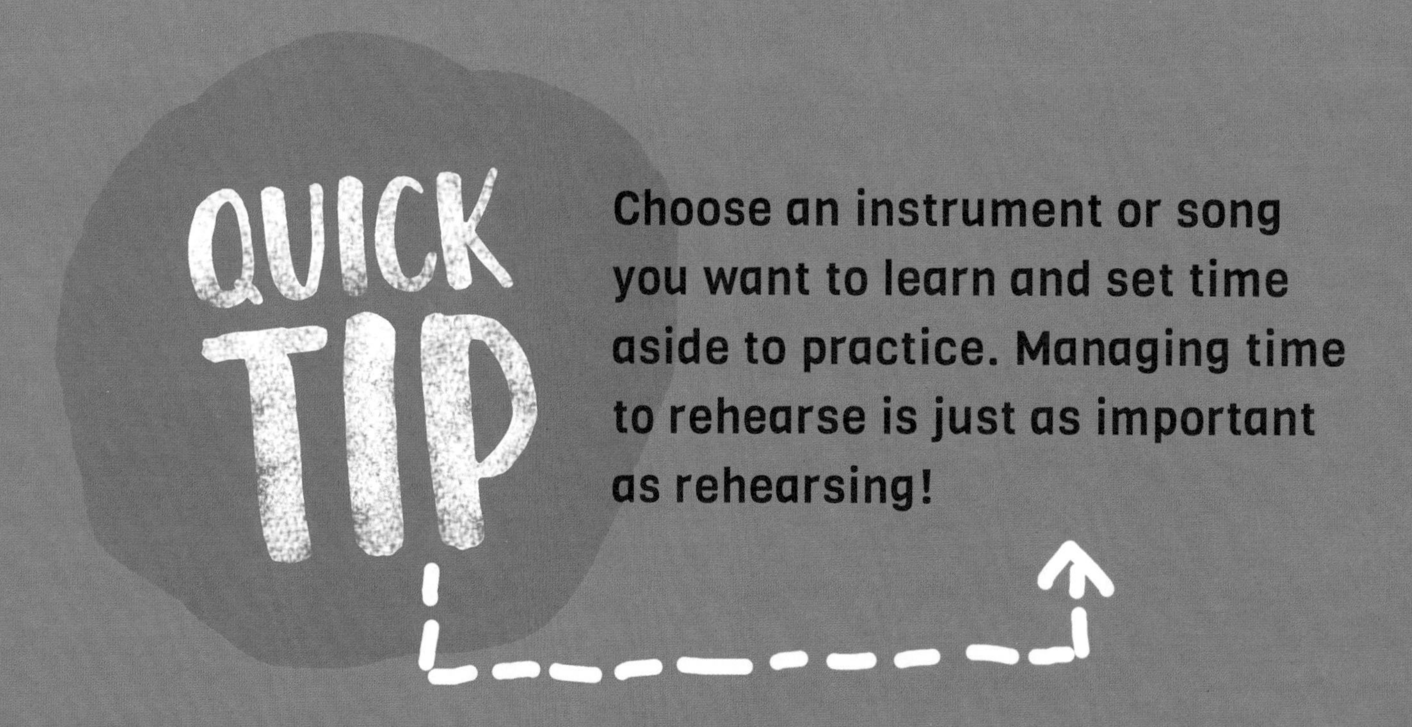

Choose an instrument or song you want to learn and set time aside to practice. Managing time to rehearse is just as important as rehearsing!

DID YOU KNOW?

Autism makes it hard for people to cope with everyday things like a loud noise or a bright light. They might find it hard to communicate how they are feeling.

The Sailor

Laura (23)

The Netherlands

SAIL AWAY!

Hi there!
I am Laura.

Laura loves the ocean.

Laura was born in New Zealand to Dutch parents and she grew up on the water: swimming, playing and sailing across the seas. Laura wanted to explore all of the water that covers 70% of our earth, and she wanted to do it all by herself. She decided to sail around the world.

Laura started in Gibraltar, an island off the Spanish coast. Her trip took her two years.

During her journey, Laura slept on a damp bed and lived on rice and pasta, with cookies and pancakes as an occasional treat. She survived weeks at sea with no company — except for the ants and cockroaches. And she still had to do her homework!

In her journal, Laura writes about meeting penguins, seals, birds, whales and dolphins. She is in awe of the beauty of the natural world.

DID YOU KNOW?

Do you know the difference between a mile and a nautical mile? We use 'nautical mile' when we reference the distance traveled across the sea. A nautical mile is much longer than a mile.

The Inventor

Lily (16), United States

LIGHT BULB MOMENT

Hi! My name is Lily.

When Lily was eight years old, she came up with an idea that changed her grandfather's life... and would change the lives of many others, too.

Lily's grandfather has Parkinson's Disease. Lily noticed her grandfather was shaking a lot. One of the symptoms for people with Parkinson's Disease is that their hands shake, which makes it hard to hold everyday things like pencils, cups, knives and forks.

Lily saw her grandfather spilled his coffee every time he drank from his cup. She wanted to help make drinking easier for him.

So Lily invented a cup she calls the Kangaroo Cup. The Kangaroo Cup has legs so it can stand strong. This means it is easier to drink from, even if you have shaky hands. Thousands of Lily's Kangaroo Cups have now been made and are used by people all around the world.

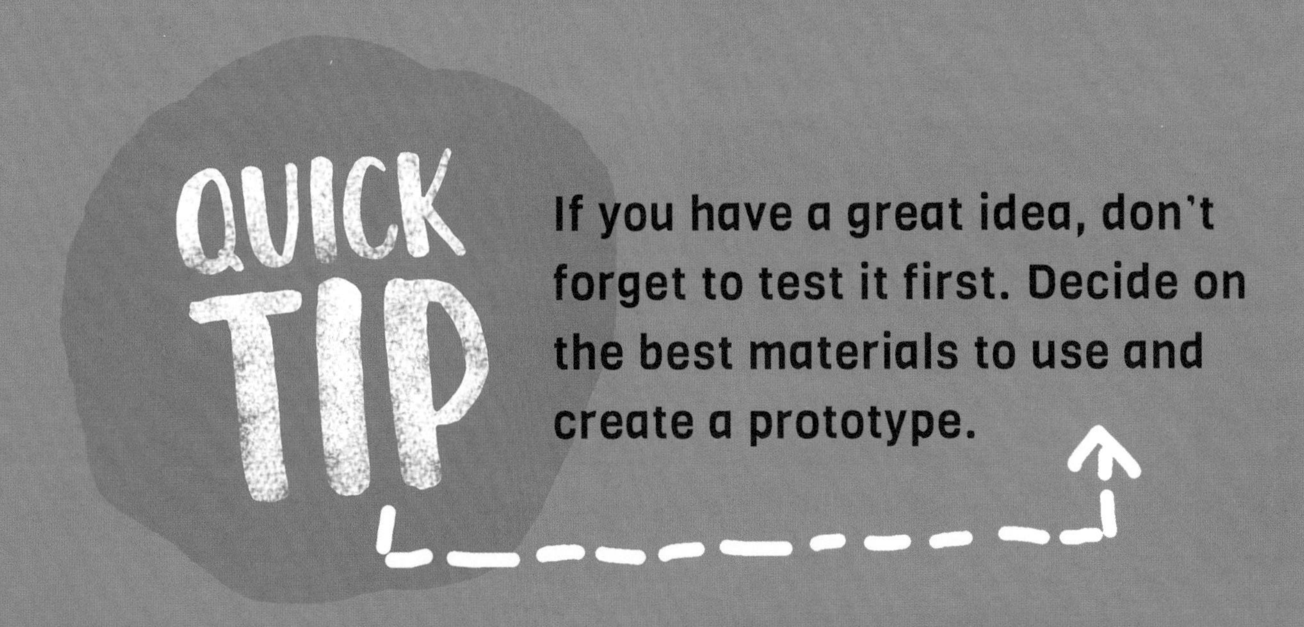

If you have a great idea, don't forget to test it first. Decide on the best materials to use and create a prototype.

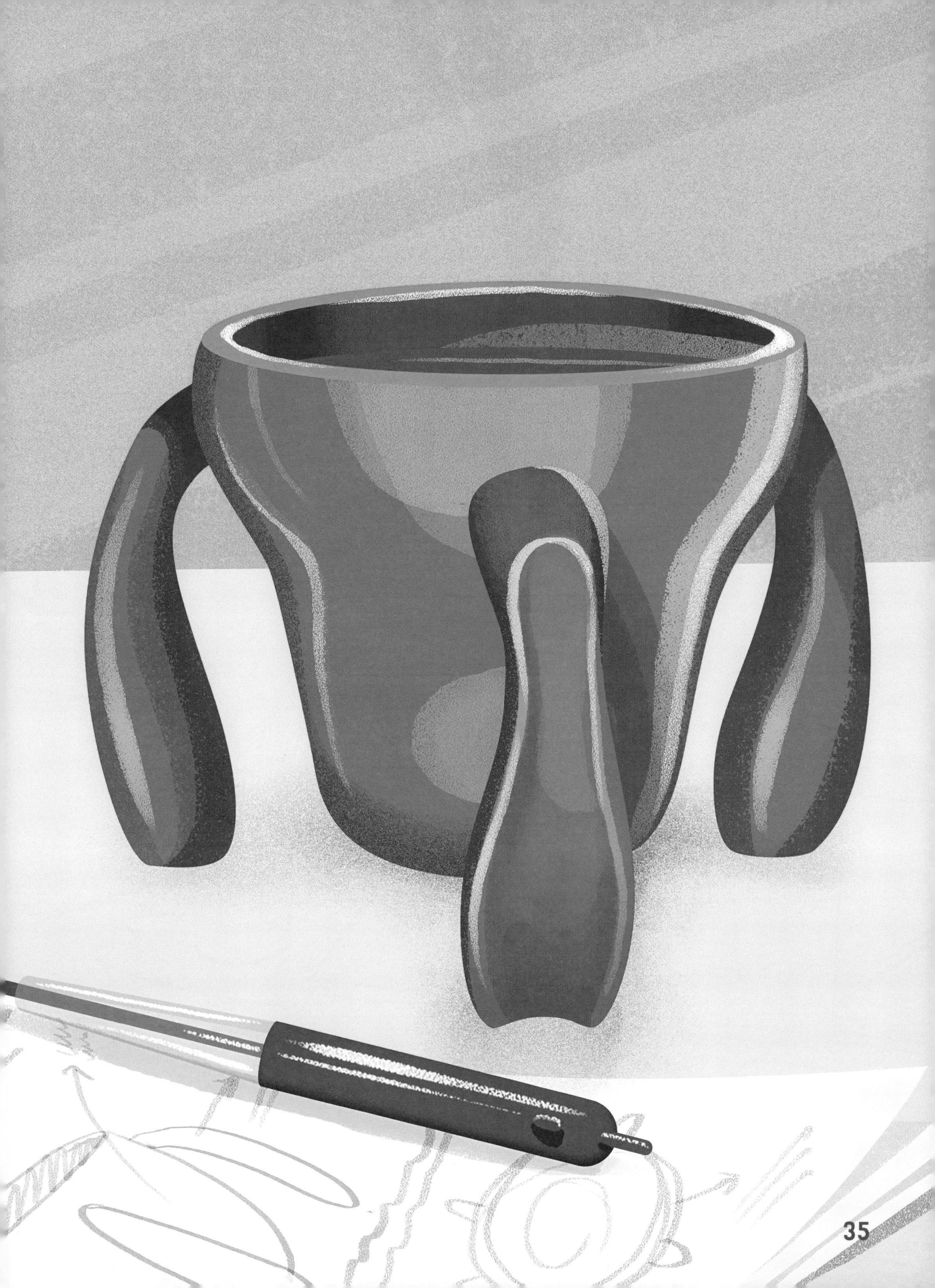

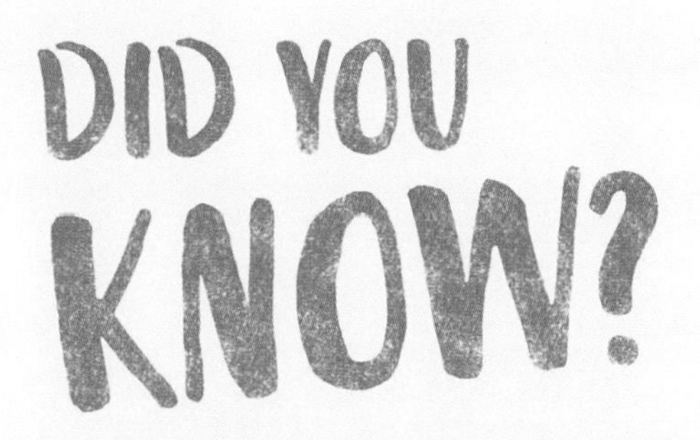

A girl named Becky is the youngest girl to have a registered invention. When she was only twelve years old, Becky invented The Glo Sheet, which allows you to do your homework in the dark!

The Water Warrior

Autumn (13), Canada

WHERE YOUR HEART IS

Hi there! I am Autumn.

Autumn is from Canada, where she lives on an indigenous reserve called Wikwemikong First Nation.

On the reserve, Autumn and her family believe water is sacred. Autumn reminds people that when we are born into this world, water has broken and 'new life is born', and so water must be valued and respected. Autumn can drink fresh water from the lake where she lives, but for many people around the world, clean water is very hard to come by. Water is one of the most important natural resources on earth. We need it for almost everything we do: washing, cooking and feeding plants.

That's one of the reasons Autumn is so passionate about protecting water. She works to prevent corporations from dumping toxic waste into the water, which makes the water unsafe to use. "We all have a right to this water as we need it — not just rich people, all people," Autumn says. Protecting water is part of protecting the earth.

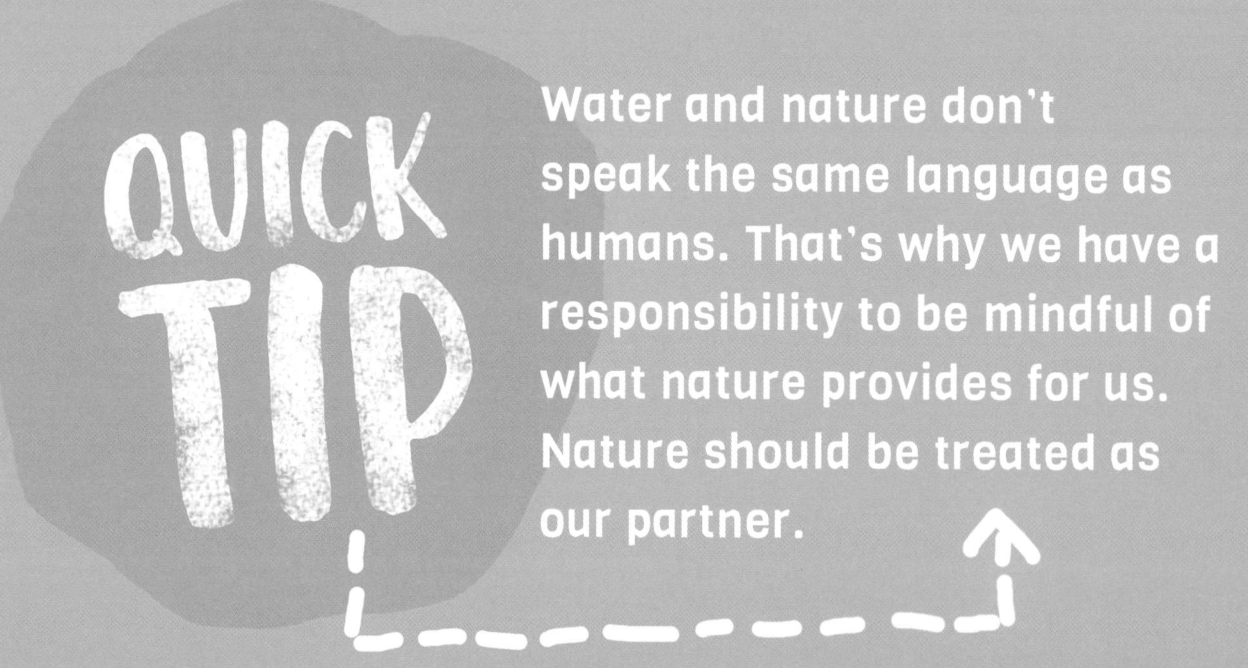

Water and nature don't speak the same language as humans. That's why we have a responsibility to be mindful of what nature provides for us. Nature should be treated as our partner.

DID YOU KNOW?
More than 1 billion people in the world don't have access to clean water.

The Survivor

Halima (15), Malawi

SAVED BY THE BELL

Hello! I am Halima.

Halima lives in Malawi with her brother and sister. Both Halima's parents have died, so the two sisters and their brother live with their grandmother. Halima's grandmother did not have enough money to buy new clothes. There was not enough food to have breakfast before going to school. At school, there were no pens or notebooks.

When she was fifteen, Halima was told to marry a man who was twice her age. She saw a man standing under a tree one day when she was walking home from school. That's when her grandmother told her he would be her husband.

Halima was not happy being married. Married life was difficult: she lived in a village without her family and friends. She was no longer allowed to go to school and spent her time cooking, cleaning and fetching water. One day she heard a group of women in her village talking about helping girls like her. They had come to help Halima go back to school.

Halima is now back at school and lives at home again, with her grandmother, her sister and her brother. She dreams of one day becoming Malawi's Minister of Education.

If you want to help other kids go to school, you can raise awareness in your community, raise funds to send more kids to school, or send backpacks and books.

School

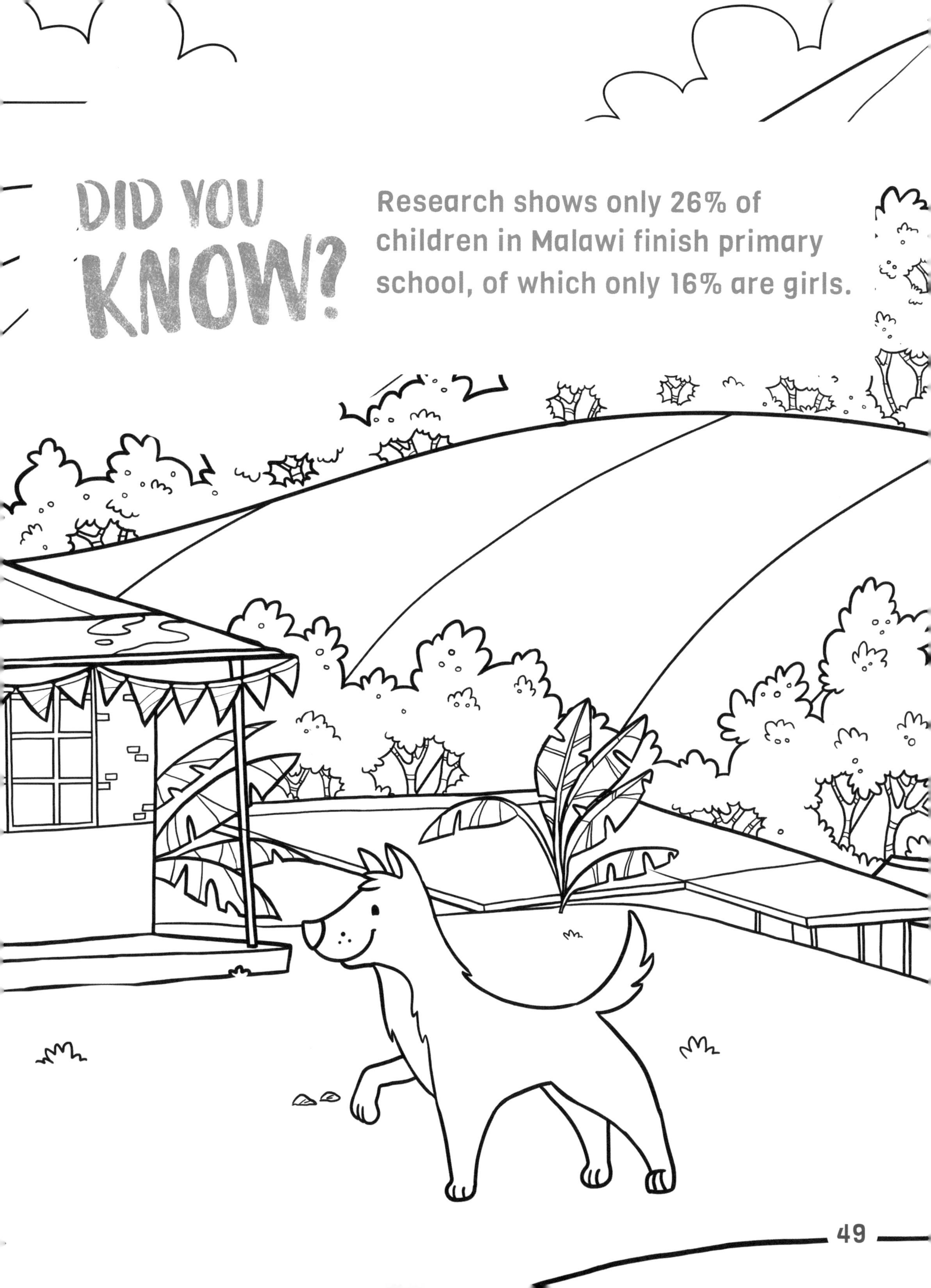

DID YOU KNOW?

Research shows only 26% of children in Malawi finish primary school, of which only 16% are girls.

The Revolutionaire

Zahra (23), The United Arab Emirates

RE-WRITING THE RULES

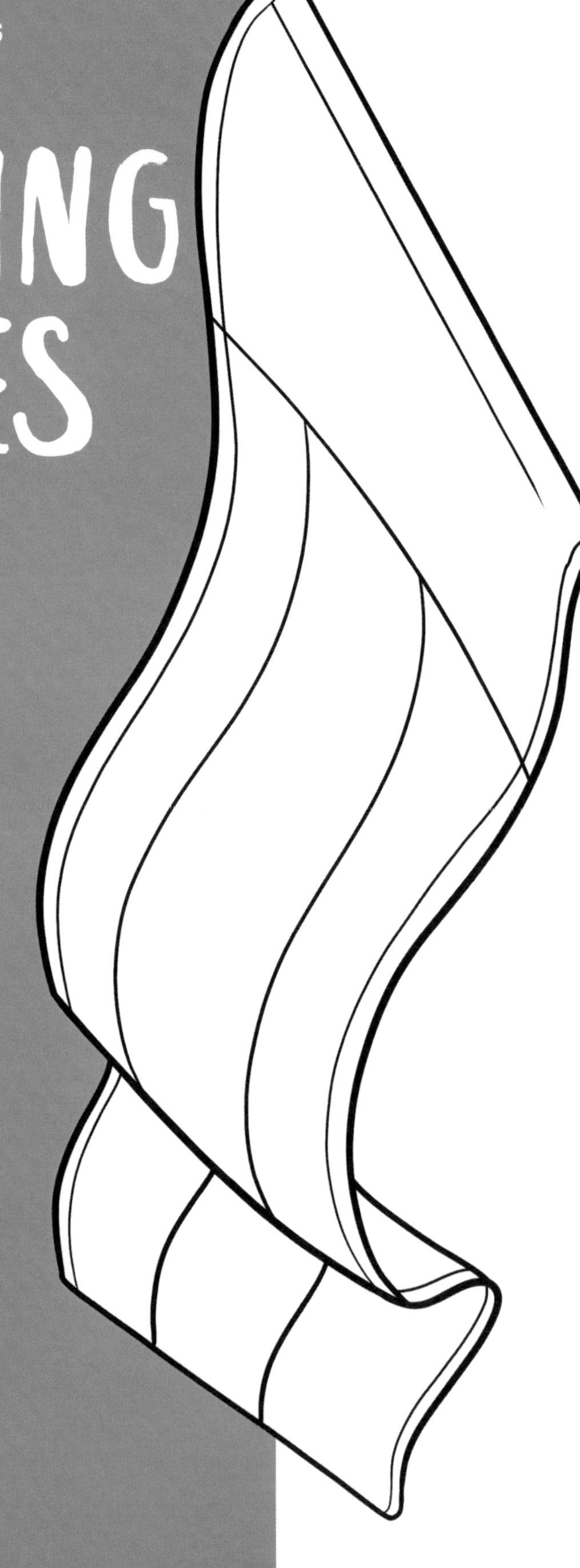

Hello! My name is Zahra.

Zahra lives in the United Arab Emirates — a country in the Middle East that mostly consists of a sandy desert landscape.

Despite the hot sun beaming down every day and the lack of snow, Zahra is a figure skater and spends her day whizzing around on her skates. Ten years after she first put on a pair of skates, she has become an international competitor. But not only that, Zahra has successfully advocated for women throughout the world to be able to compete on a global sports stage — no matter what they choose to wear.

Zahra chooses to express her identity and religion by wearing a headscarf. She has gained the respect and understanding of the sports authorities and has made invaluable changes to the judging criteria in figure skating competitions. Thanks to her work, there are no longer dress code deductions for Muslim competitors wearing the headscarf.

Zahra does not want to compromise what she believes in in order to do what she loves. Zahra believes all girls and young women should find their passion and not let small obstacles feel like mountains.

QUICK TIP

If something doesn't make you feel comfortable, speak up against it. There will always be someone out there who feels the same way you do.

DID YOU KNOW?

For a very long time, women in some countries were not allowed to wear trousers in public.

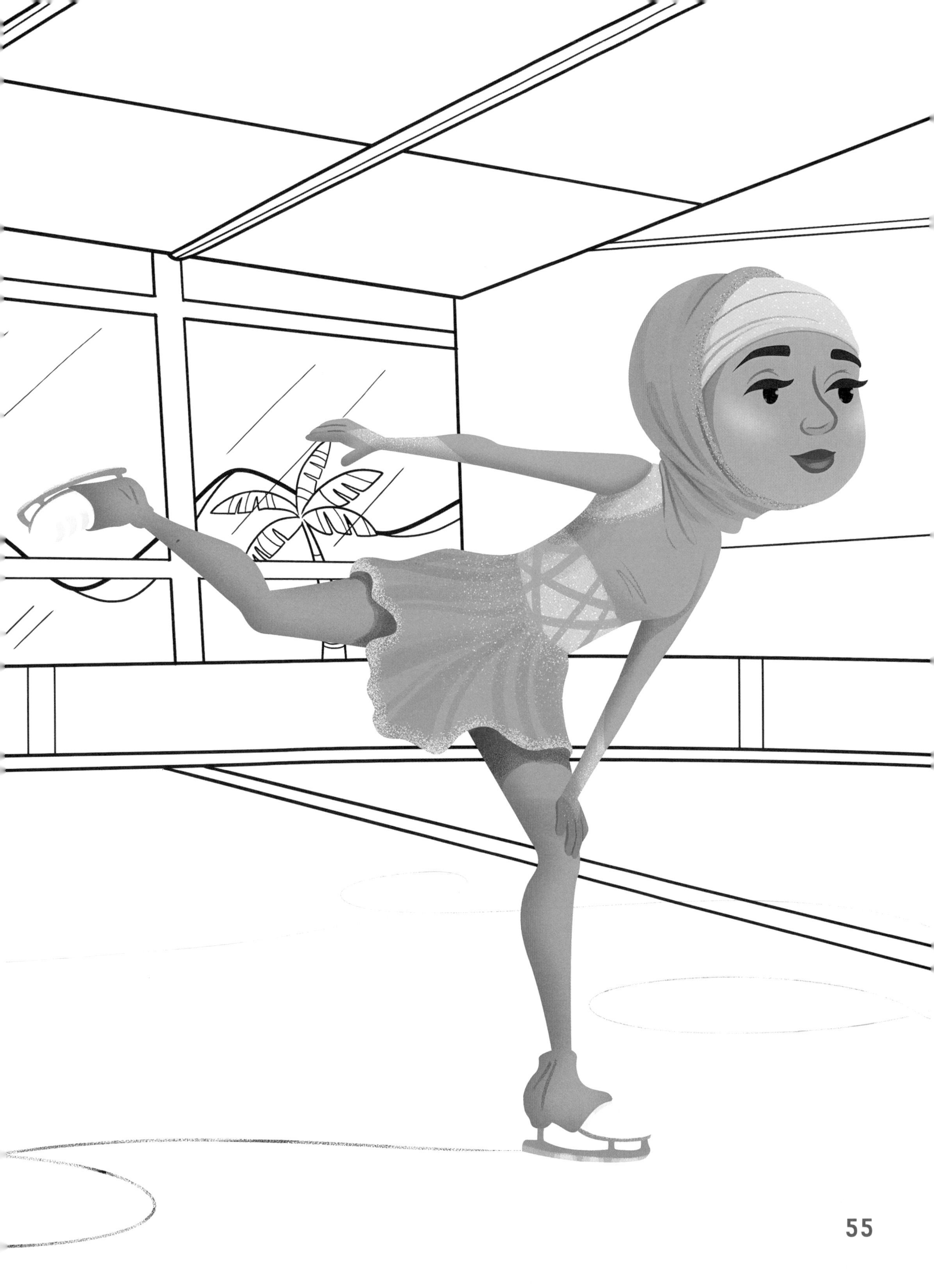

The Surfer

Zahlia (12), Australia

RIDING YOUR WAVE

Hi! I am Zahlia.

Zahlia has been surfing since she was four years old. She loves to surf and paddles out on the water with her sister. The sisters can be competitive, but what's most important to them is spending time together while doing a sport they love.

What Zahlia loves about being on the water is that she feels at one with nature — she can embrace what nature provides. Surfing gives her an escape from the world around her and she can focus on being herself.

Zahlia is dedicated to being the best she can be at surfing and practices every week. She says, "Surfing provides a feeling like no other — it's almost like the more hard work you put in, the bigger the reward from Mother Nature!"

Surfing isn't always easy — the competition can be fierce. Zahlia stays motivated because she gets stronger after every challenge she faces and is focused on her goal of one day becoming a World Title Surfer.

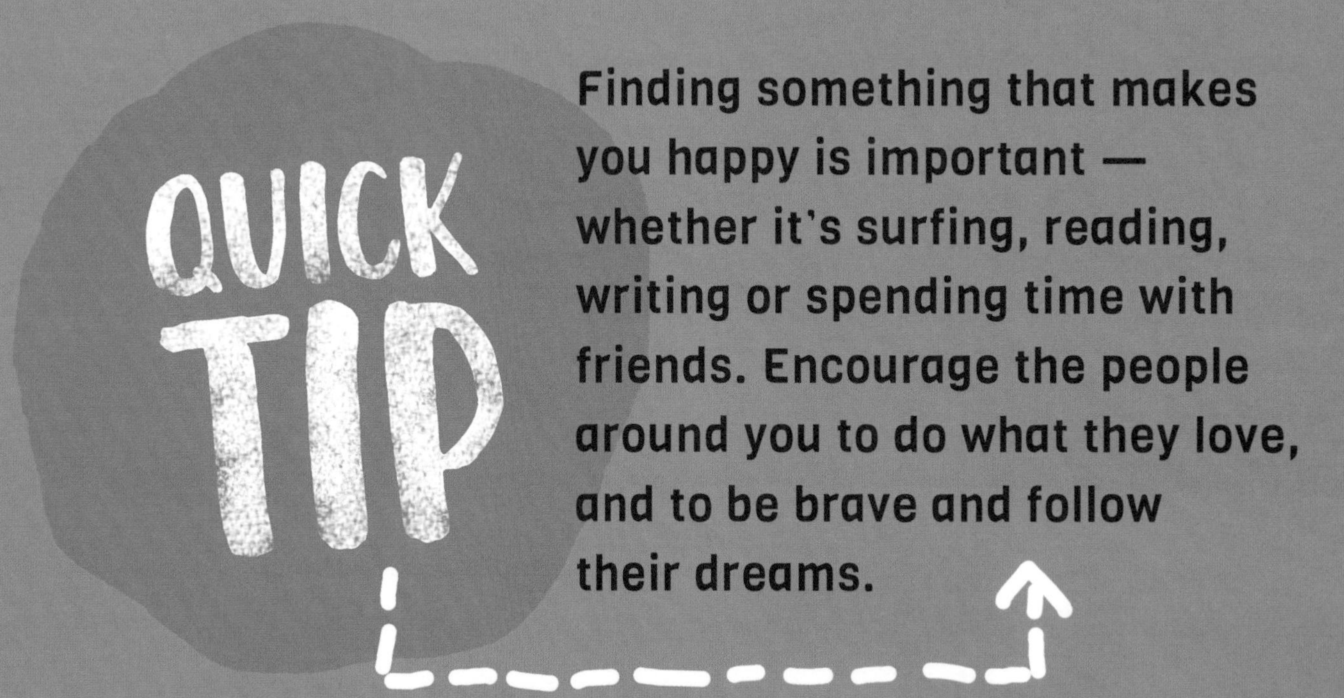

Finding something that makes you happy is important — whether it's surfing, reading, writing or spending time with friends. Encourage the people around you to do what they love, and to be brave and follow their dreams.

DID YOU KNOW?

Surfing is one of the oldest sports on earth. Though we don't know exactly when people started to surf, 5,000-year-old prehistoric stone carvings from Peru show people surfing.

The Activist

April (19), Colombia

THE COLORS OF DIVERSITY

Hello! I am April.

THE COLORS OF DIVERSITY

April is from Colombia where she is studying at university. Throughout her life, April felt different — she was born a boy, and now chooses to live as a girl. For many people, this is hard to understand — they don't believe people should choose to be different.

Now, April is passionate about fighting for human diversity. Diversity means we honor and celebrate strengths, differences and similarities across all people. Every day, April reminds people around her that it's okay to be different and that it's okay to imagine a better world.

It's not always easy to fight for a cause that's hard for other people to understand. April encourages people to continue to speak up about things that are important to them.

THE COLORS OF DIVERSITY

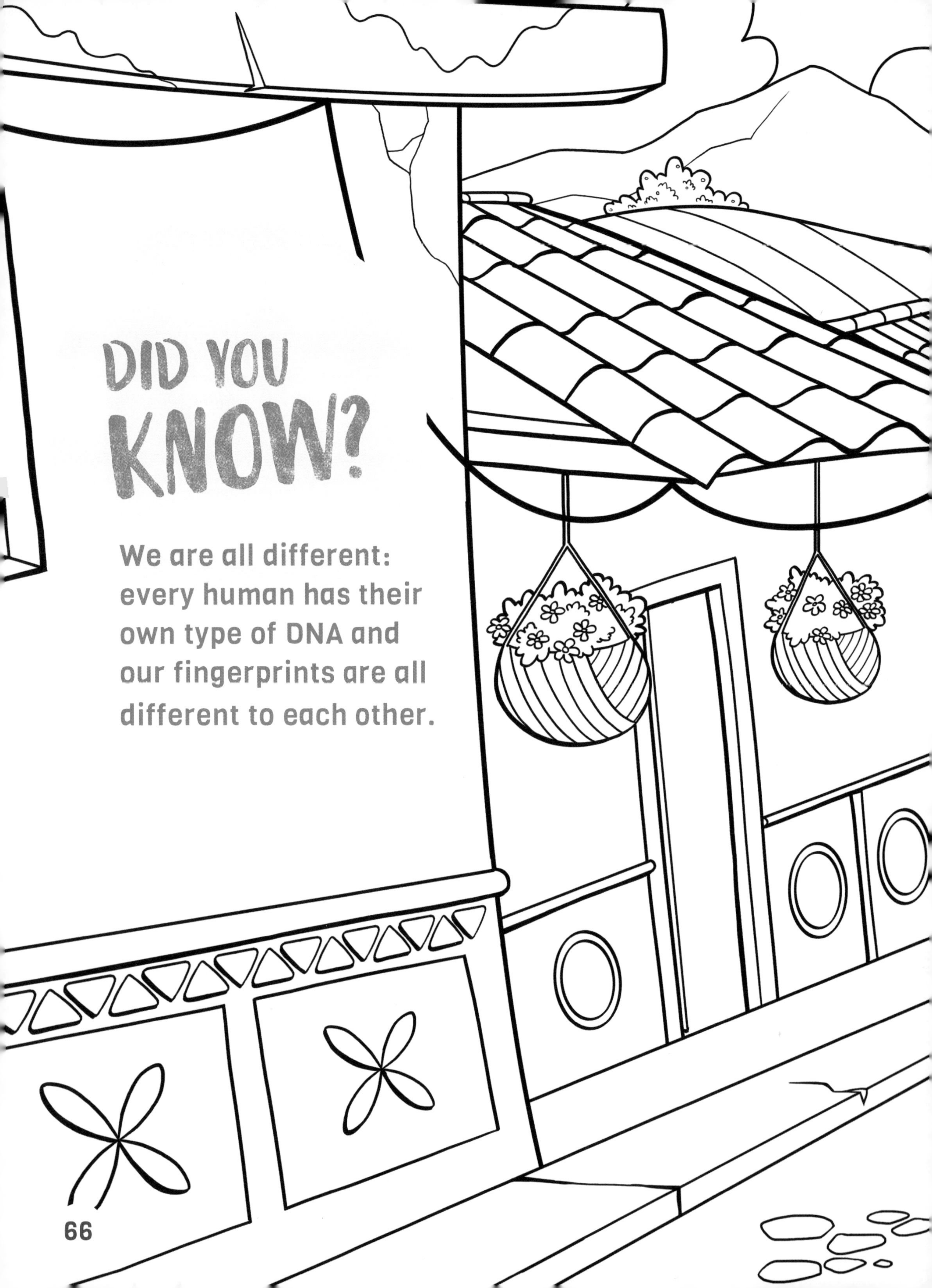

DID YOU KNOW?

We are all different: every human has their own type of DNA and our fingerprints are all different to each other.

The Groundbreaker

Ayane (23), Japan

CHANGE-OVER

Hello!
I am Ayane.

ラグビー

When Ayane was ten years old, she saw her brother play rugby. Ayane immediately knew she wanted to play rugby, too. But in Japan there wasn't a girls' rugby team. So Ayane joined the boys' team.

When Ayane was playing, she got bullied. She was made fun of and she thought, "I will never succeed." She sometimes asked herself why she was playing rugby. But she didn't want to stop and she continued to follow her passion — she wanted to show others that girls can play rugby, too.

Ayane's playing got better and better. She was so good that she was chosen to go to Australia on a special program for sports stars. Ayane spoke about her first few months in a new country: "It wasn't so easy, I could not make friends. My English wasn't good, it was so hard to communicate. I felt ashamed but I did not give up. I just tried my best all the time." Now Ayane is one of the best-known female Japanese rugby players in Australia!

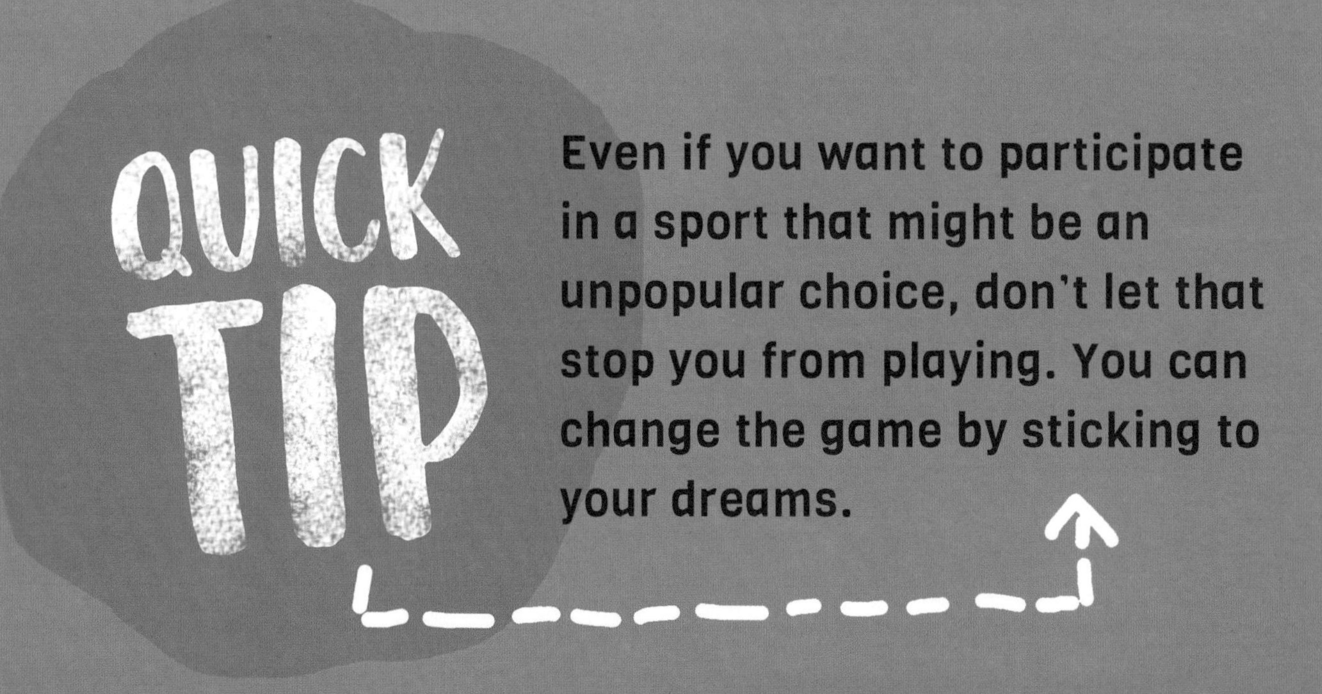

Even if you want to participate in a sport that might be an unpopular choice, don't let that stop you from playing. You can change the game by sticking to your dreams.

ラグビーボール

DID YOU KNOW?

To be a good athlete, it's important to train your mind, as well as your body. Being mentally prepared to play your best game is key!

The Techies

Coding Girls, Afghanistan

CODE TO INSPIRE

Hello! We are the Afghan Coding Girls.

In Afghanistan, a group of young women are writing code in order to create a video game. The video game supports Afghanistan's efforts to prevent farmland being used to grow opium. Opium is used to make illegal drugs.

One of the coders, Khatera, explained the game was based on her brother's experience as a translator in the south of Afghanistan. "Each time he came back home, he would tell us about the poppy fields, the terrible mine blasts, battling opium traffickers and drugs," Khatera said.

That is why, together with her classmates, she decided a computer game could bring attention to the issue, especially amongst young people. It could be their way to help in the fight against opium.

In the game, the player's mission is to clear the area of drugs and to use the land to grow a crop like saffron instead. The soldier faces problems in the process: enemies hiding in tall corn fields, land mines, drug traffickers and hidden laboratories.

QUICK TIP

One of the best ways to learn how to code is to learn by doing. You can start your own personal coding project to perfect your skills.

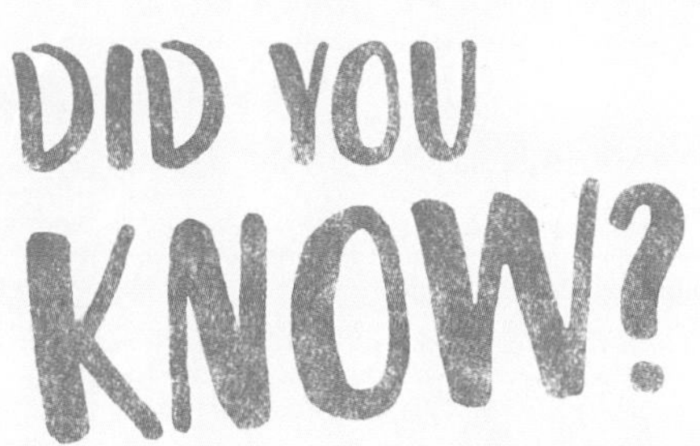

In the mid-1800s, Ada Lovelace translated 'instructions' for the first computer program — making her one of the world's first coders.

LEARN MOR

→ The Environmentalists

To learn more about Isabel and Melati's work,
visit: www.byebyeplasticbags.org

→ The Singer

To support Ashleigh's singing and her dream to meet Ed Sheeran, visit: www.facebook.com/public/Ashleigh-Fagan

→ The Sailor

To read more about Laura's journey,
visit: www.lauradekker.nl/English/About_Laura.html

→ The Inventor

To buy a Kangaroo Cup,
visit: www.imagiroo.com/about

The Water Warrior

To support Autumn's work,
visit: www.facebook.com/Waterwarrior1

The Survivor

To support Halima and other girls like her,
visit: https://letgirlslearn.gov

The Revolutionaire

To learn more about Zahra,
visit: www.facebook.com/ZahraSkate

The Surfer

To learn more about Zahlia,
visit: www.surfgirlmag.com

The Activist

To learn more about April,
visit: www.mujeresalborde.org/mujeres-al-borde/nosotrs

The Groundbreaker

To learn more about Ayane,
visit: www.women2watch.net/2017/04/05/girls-to-watch-ayane-hirata

The Techies

To learn more about Code to Inspire,
visit: www.codetoinspire.org

THE ENVIRONMENTALISTS

How many ways can you think of to clean up the environment around you? What are easy ways you can use less plastic?

MY SPACE TO CREATE

THE SINGER

Music allows us to express our thoughts and communicate what we are feeling. How many ways of communicating can you think of? Why do you think singing, dancing and drawing are all considered ways to communicate?

MY SPACE TO CREATE

THE SAILOR

What would you enjoy most about sailing around the world? What do you think you would discover and what, if anything, do you think you might be afraid of?

MY SPACE TO CREATE

THE INVENTOR

If you could invent anything in the world, what would you invent? What kind of impact would your invention have?

MY SPACE TO CREATE

THE WATER WARRIOR

How many ways can you think of that would allow us to help save water? Why do you think it's important to respect nature around us?

MY SPACE TO CREATE

THE SURVIVOR

Can you think of two things you like about school? Maybe it's seeing your friends or leaning a new language. What is your favorite part of the school day?

MY SPACE TO CREATE

THE REVOLUTIONAIRE

If you could change one rule for children around the world, what would that rule be?

MY SPACE TO CREATE

THE SURFER

How many things can you think of that make you happy? How can you inspire others to be happy and to follow their passion?

MY SPACE TO CREATE

THE GROUNDBREAKER

Do you think it's fair that some sports are considered 'boy' sports and others are considered 'girl' sports? Why or why not?

MY SPACE TO CREATE

THE TECHIES

If you could create any computer game, what kind of computer game would you create? Why might you like to learn how to code?

MY SPACE TO CREATE

ABOUT THE

THE CHANGEMAKER

Jos loves to be creative! She was born in Brazil and has traveled around the world (to almost 100 countries) and loves learning about different cultures, people and places. She has spent her life acting and singing on stage, reading books, playing sports and working in human rights. She loves working on exciting, world-changing projects with inspiring people.

THE BOOK QUEEN

Kira lives in a home where the books are piled so high they almost reach the ceiling! She has been reading and writing books since she was a little girl, and is the founder of The Dreamwork Collective, an independent publisher dedicated to sharing diverse voices and powerful stories. She helps creatives and visionaries — just like you — do their dream work in the world.

TEAM

THE CREATIVE THINKER

Jade has always loved creating, from drawing portraits to making things that move. She likes to calculate and solve problems and believes that her purpose is to improve education using her creative and problem solving superpowers. Being in nature makes her feel energized and her favorite place to be is the ocean. Jade knows that every single person has a talent that can be used for doing good.

THE ARTIST

Bianca started going to art class in Cape Town, South Africa — where she is from — when she was only four years old. Since then, she knew that when she grew up, she wanted to be an artist. She loves to draw and she loves spending time with her friends and family. Bianca thinks the most important thing in improving your drawing skills is to never stop practicing!